Let us try an experiment to show one of the most mysterious things about the mind — the *imagination*.

Try closing your eyes and imagining that you are standing on a beautiful, clean, sandy beach, looking out over the ocean. In the far distance, almost a speck on the horizon, you can see a ship. Think of how many miles you would have to go to travel all that distance! Yet you made a complete picture of it in your mind. You can even imagine that you are hearing the waves breaking on the beach, and can feel the cool ocean breeze on your face. The human mind can create anything in the imagination. And who can truly say which is more real, the actual ocean or the ocean in your mind?

In this book we will explore some of the mysterious workings of the mind. First, we will look at *the study of the mind*, from the ancient sciences of astrology, medicine and philosophy to the newer science of psychology. We will learn a little about *the parts of the mind*, and what makes people so very different in the way they think, feel and behave. We will talk a little about that very mysterious centre of the mind, the real 'I', which some psychologists call the *Self*. And we will explore some of the ways in which we can become more aware of who we really are. We might call this section pathways into the mind. This book can only be a beginning, because there is so much we do not understand about the mind. But learning as much as we can about it means learning about ourselves and other people. And that is an important part of what life is about.

The study of the mind

Socrates

We now call the science of studying the mind *psychology*. This word comes from two Greek words, *logos* which means wisdom or knowledge, and *psyche* which means soul. The earliest psychologists were the ancient philosophers, who sought to understand the mind of man by understanding how he related to the cosmos, or God. Pythagoras the ancient Greek thinker whose work forms the basis of our study of geometry, believed that both man and the universe were built upon the same basic laws or principles. Socrates, another Greek philosopher, believed that man's mind was in touch with the divine and that true education really meant bringing forth all the inner wisdom contained in the mind rather than feeding it with facts. Plato, who was a pupil of Socrates, believed that everything we experience in life comes from certain basic ideas or patterns which exist in the mind of God. Aristotle, who was Plato's student, was perhaps the first man to record the wisdom of these earlier teachers in a psychological system. These great men have contributed much to our understanding of the mind.

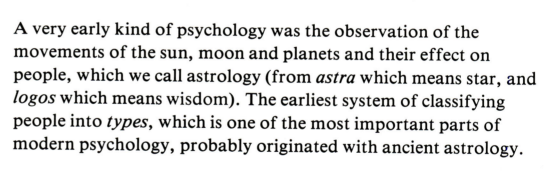

Plato

A very early kind of psychology was the observation of the movements of the sun, moon and planets and their effect on people, which we call astrology (from *astra* which means star, and *logos* which means wisdom). The earliest system of classifying people into *types*, which is one of the most important parts of modern psychology, probably originated with ancient astrology.

Ancient medicine also explored the human mind. Doctors in ancient times were concerned with treating the whole man, instead of just one sick part of his body. They believed that disease was really 'dis-ease', which meant that a man was not at ease with himself. Today modern medicine is beginning to recognise this ancient truth, and so today we have a branch of medicine called *psychosomatic* medicine which studies the effect of the mind on the body.

Until the 16th century, man continued to view himself as part of a

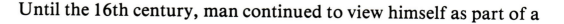

Looking at
THE MIND

Liz Greene

Coventure

Printed by W S Cowell Ltd,
Ipswich, Suffolk, England
First published in the UK 1977
by Coventure Ltd, London, England
ISBN 0 904576 41 8

Introduction

Do you ever wonder what makes you especially you, and different from everyone else? When you say, 'I am happy', or 'I am sad', have you ever asked who it is that is happy or sad? Who is 'I'?

When you are thinking about that question, you are using your mind. It is the mind which tell us how we feel, and causes us to think and act differently from every other living thing.

The mind is not the same thing as the brain, which is part of the body. Modern science is learning a lot about how the brain works, and it is a fascinating subject. The brain is like a central telephone exchange. There are inside lines to the digestive system, nervous system, heart, lungs and other parts of the body which we don't think about. These lines are called the *autonomic nervous system* (from two Greek words, *auto* meaning by itself, and *nomos* meaning law). Through other inside lines we can control our speech and movements. There are outside lines through the senses — sight, hearing, touch, taste and smell — to the outside world.

But for all we are learning about the brain, we still do not understand what the human mind is. We might say that the mind is *consciousness*, which comes from the Latin words *con* (with) and *scire* (to know). We do not know whether this wonderful thing called consciousness, which lets me know that I am me and lets you know that you are you, is actually in the brain, or whether it is something much more mysterious that works through the brain in the same way a radio announcer will use his equipment to broadcast his messages to other people. We know a lot about the equipment, but we still do not understand who the broadcaster is.

Man's mind is the gift which makes him different from every other living thing. Animals and plants are alive and respond to the experiences of life. But as far as we know they do not understand themselves. They do not ask who 'I' is.

Paracelsus

larger cosmos. Great medieval physicians like Paracelsus studied the human mind and combined medicine with philosophy, astrology and alchemy (the beginning of the modern science of chemistry). Many great writers and artists also sought to understand the mind of man through their art.

Descartes was a great French philosopher and mathematician who lived at the beginning of the 17th Century. He thought that the body and the mind were two distinctly different things. Descartes' view of man brought to an end the old medieval view that man was a unity within himself and with the cosmos. Although this dualism of body and mind has caused many problems in the study of modern psychology, it allowed psychology to develop as a science, free from the mysticism of the Middle Ages.

After Descartes, psychology became part of the study of philosophy again. But 17th and 18th Century philosophy was very different from Greek philosophy. It lacked the feeling of the inner dignity and divinity of the human soul. This period of history is known as the Age of Enlightenment, because man felt he had outgrown the superstitions and childlike beliefs of the Middle Ages. He believed that the intellect was the greatest gift of the mind.

In the 19th Century many new discoveries were made about the human brain and body. With these new discoveries, psychology became more and more influenced by medicine.

The first laboratory of experimental psychology was founded by Wilhelm Wundt in Germany in 1879. This was the real beginning of the study of psychology as a science. Wundt was especially interested in memory and in how the brain influenced body reactions.

Wilhelm Wundt

Psychology during the 19th Century became more and more a branch of biology. It was also influenced by Darwin, whose research into the evolution of man made it necessary for psychologists to study animals as well as human beings.

William James, a great American psychologist who lived in the second half of the 19th Century, contributed much to modern psychology by his study of *consciousness*. He felt that consciousness, or awareness, was important in itself, and should be studied independent of the body processes which accompanied it.

Pavlov also contributed much to modern psychology. He was especially interested in *conditioned reflexes*. A conditioned reflex is a response which has become a habit because a person, or an animal, has learned to react in a certain way over and over again to something happening outside him. Pavlov's work with dogs has shown us that in many ways we are very influenced by our environments.

Anton Mesmer

One of the first pioneers who used his knowledge of the mind to heal illness was Anton Mesmer, who lived in the 19th century. Mesmer probably used what we now call *hypnotism* by finding that, when he produced a certain sleeplike state in his patients, he could get them to heal their bodies with their minds in a way which seemed miraculous to other doctors of his time.

One of the greatest founders of modern psychology was Sigmund Freud, who was a medical doctor. His discoveries about parts of the mind which are hidden or *unconscious* completely changed man's view of himself. Although many of Freud's theories may now seem outdated to some psychologists, we owe him a great deal because he established the study of the mind as a science and proved that it is possible for there to be many hidden things in a person's mind which can influence his behaviour and feelings without his realising it.

Sigmund Freud

Sigmund Freud founded the school of psychology called *psychoanalysis*. Although he was a doctor, and studied the workings of the body, his work differed from other psychologists' because he was especially interested in the abnormal mind.

Alfred Adler

Roberto Assagioli

Carl Jung

For many years after Freud began his work, psychology was a science which worked exclusively to heal people who suffered in their minds. This study is now called *psychiatry*. Some great psychiatrists like Adler, Jones and Reich worked to find out why the mind seemed to cause sickness in some people.

Other pioneers in the field of psychology began to become interested in the healthy mind and in the creative powers of the mind. They discovered that sometimes what seems like a sickness in the mind is really a sign that the mind is trying to grow and to resolve a problem which the person does not yet realize. Men like Carl Jung, Abraham Maslow, Carl Rogers and Roberto Assagioli studied this field. One of the most important ideas which Jung developed is that the mind of man seeks growth and understanding as one of its natural needs, just as a plant seeks sunlight.

Since Jung's work, modern psychologists are realizing that although it is very important to help people to adjust better to the society they live in, it is also very important to help them discover what is special and individual within them so that they can be true to themselves.

There are many different schools of thought within the field of psychology, and sometimes they do not agree with each other. But all of them contribute something of value to our understanding. We all have many different aspects to our minds, and each branch of psychology tells us about a different aspect. Although psychologists often quarrel with each other, it is probable that no one school of psychology is "better" than another. If we really wish to understand a little of the wonder and greatness of the mind, we must learn something about each different psychological school.

These are the different fields of human activity that psychology studies.

Comparative psychology studies the relationship between animal and human behaviour.

Genetic psychology studies the differences between people based on the hereditary abilities and traits with which they are born.

Abnormal psychology studies mental illness, and is primarily a part of the study of medicine.

Social psychology studies the workings of the social group, and the psychological side of social values and standards.

Industrial psychology studies the psychology of industry, and the needs of the individual in his work life. It is concerned with the psychological side of management, labour, and relationships between employer and employee.

Educational psychology studies the development of the child in school, and the ways in which he learns.

Clinical psychology studies the techniques of counselling and psychotherapy, and the ways in which an individual can seek guidance and help for his problems.

Another way of looking at psychology is to divide it into four great streams of thought. These four streams all explore different aspects of the human being.

Behavioural psychology is the study of the person in relation to his environment. It is concerned with how we can learn to free ourselves from patterns which we have learned very early in life which hurt us. A keyword for behavioural psychology is *adjustment*. It studies how we adjust to our families, to our schools, to our society, and to life around us.

Depth psychology studies the very deep levels of the emotions, and explores all the secret and hidden areas of the mind by looking at dreams and fantasies. A keyword for depth psychology is *motive,* and the depth psychologist is more interested in *why* we behave in a certain way than in *how* we behave. Freud's school of *psychoanalysis* and Jung's school of *analytical psychology* are the two main schools within the stream of depth psychology.

Humanistic psychology studies how people relate to each other in groups, and how they can communicate better with each other. Humanistic psychology is especially valuable in education, industry, and other areas where people must learn to relate to each other. A keyword for humanistic psychology is *relationship,* and most of the techniques used by the humanistic psychologist are concerned with growth through contact and exchange with others.

Transpersonal psychology studies the very special and important part of the mind which is connected with spiritual beliefs, and with man's need for a deep inner experience of his own soul. A transpersonal psychologist may work with techniques and ideas belonging to all the different schools of psychology, but he is concerned more with the inner purpose of the person's life. A keyword for transpersonal psychology is *meaning.* Regardless of whether we are well-adjusted to society, able to make good relationships with those around us, and know something about our own motives, we must still feel there is some meaning to our lives. In some ways this stream of psychology is the most important of all, for a man can endure almost anything, and can achieve almost anything, if he has an inner sense of purpose.

The parts of the mind

We can now find out a little about how the different parts of the mind work and speak to each other, and how they are related to the centre or core of each person. We can also find out something about the basic ways in which we relate to life and people.

Conscious and Unconscious

Although we cannot really divide the mind into sections, many psychologists talk about two different levels of the mind, called the *conscious* and the *unconscious*. A good way of picturing these levels would be to imagine the mind as something like an iceberg. A small part — the conscious — shows above the surface of the water. But most of the iceberg is hidden beneath the water, and we cannot see it. We need to learn something about this hidden part, for otherwise it can sometimes be a hazard, in the same way that the hidden base of an iceberg is a hazard to a ship.

The conscious is the part of the mind which is aware of things at any given time. When you know something like your friend's birthday, you are conscious of it. There are some things we are always conscious of — such as our names, or where we live. Other things are sometimes conscious and then we forget them. The conscious mind stops working when we are asleep, and resumes work when we awaken. As we grow older, the conscious mind becomes filled with more and more understanding as we learn more things and see more of life.

The unconscious is much more mysterious, because it contains all those parts of the person of which he is not aware. Some of these things are memories which we have forgotten. They have 'gone somewhere', but we know they can be remembered if we learn how. For example, can you remember being born? Most people cannot. Yet you were there at the time! And psychologists have proven that a person can be taught to remember the experience of birth.

The collective unconscious is a storehouse of human experience from the dawn of time right up through all the eras of history into the present. And who knows? Perhaps it contains the seeds of the future as well.

There are deeper layers in the unconscious. Many of the talents and abilities which appear later in life exist in the unconscious and are waiting for the person to develop to a point where he can use them. The person you are growing into already exists in a sort of rough sketch or basic blueprint in the unconscious. This is why it is so important for us to be true to ourselves, for we are already individuals from the moment of our birth. We must learn to follow this blueprint whether other people approve of it or not. It is like the acorn which can eventually become an oak tree. The future of the oak tree is contained in the acorn, yet it needs time and the proper growing conditions to follow its blueprint. In many ways the unconscious contains a lot of wisdom, because sometimes our conscious minds cannot really see where we are going.

There is also a very, very deep layer of the unconscious which is called the *collective* unconscious. This contains memories of all mankind's experiences throughout the ages. We all have the same heritage, because we are all human beings. And there are some experiences, such as birth, love, fear, conflict, growth and death which all people share. The collective unconscious contains memories of all these things and there is a lot of wisdom in so many thousands of years of experience.

It is thought that these memories may be contained in the structure of the human brain itself, so that with the birth of the body we come into life with an unconscious awareness of all the most important experiences. This may be something like *instinct*, which allows birds to know how to migrate without anybody ever showing them, and allows bees to build hives without previous instruction. With man, however, it is not only biological instincts that are inherited, but perhaps ideas and feelings as well. The process of living gradually awakens these memories or instincts, so that with every important experience in life we are acting creatively as individuals and also acting out an age-old story.

We are only just beginning to learn what the unconscious is really about. It is not only a place where painful or unpleasant things are stored. It is also a wonderful part of the mind which contains our real creative potential and the secret of our real identity. The process of living is also a process of gradually becoming more and more conscious of everything we are and have always been without realizing it.

Extraverts and Introverts

We can take people and divide them into two groups. *Extraverted* people (from the Latin *extra*, meaning outside, and *vertere*, to turn) are interested in other people, action, and the world around them. They want to live life to the fullest. They like to have lots of people around them, make friends easily, and don't enjoy being alone. *Introverted* people (the Latin, *intro* means inside) are usually more withdrawn and more interested in the inner thoughts and feelings which flow through their minds. It takes a long time to get to know them, and they sometimes have a secret inner world which they like a lot better than the one outside.

Extraverted boys and girls are usually well-liked and enjoy school because they can have many friends and enjoy many different activities. But introverted boys and girls are sometimes misunderstood, because they are often shy and quiet and seem as though they don't really want to be friendly. This is not really true, and they may have many deep and loving feelings and wonderful ideas locked up inside. This is why it is so important to look beneath the surface and take the time to get to know a person and see what he is really like. Being extraverted is not any better than being introverted. It is just different, and each has something to offer.

There are really four basic ways in which we relate to life through our minds. Some psychologists call these the *four functions of consciousness*.

Sensation

The simplest way we have of perceiving life is through the five senses. When you are enjoying a good meal or the feel of a beautiful object, you are using the sensation function. When you have saved your money to buy yourself something you really want, or you have organized your time in a wise and practical way, you are also using the *sensation* function, because you are acting according to the basic practical facts you have learned about life.

Sensation is also the part of us which responds to the beauty of nature and of the animal kingdom. Some people are especially gifted and sensitive in this way, and many fine artists and sculptors and also athletes have trained this function.

Thinking

Once we are aware of something, we must be able to know what it is and decide how it is different from everything else. This is using the *thinking* function. You can see this function at work when you are studying a subject like science or mathematics, where you must use logic and work according to fixed principles. There are many people who are especially gifted in thinking, and among them we can find many great philosophers, mathematicians, scientists and engineers who are interested in the underlying ideas and structures by which life functions.

Feeling

We can also understand our experiences of life through the *feeling* function. When you have a warm and happy experience of sharing love with a parent or a special pet, you are feeling. All people feel, and all people need to share their feelings with others.

Our feelings allow us to experience other people directly. We can take our experiences and make them special and personal, so that they mean something to us deep inside. Through feeling we share love, sympathy and other emotions. Feeling allows us to know that we are not alone. Many people in the healing professions, as well as many artists, poets and musicians, are very gifted in this way.

Sometimes we are taught not to show our feelings to others. But every person needs to express what he feels, whether he is happy or unhappy, angry or fearful. A long time ago it used to be thought that girls could express feeling but boys should not. It was thought unmasculine for a boy to cry or show affection or other emotions. But we know now that both boys and girls feel equally. Each of us contains a little of both men and women. It is important to explore this other side to our natures, because then people of the opposite sex do not seem so strange or difficult to understand.

Intuition

The fourth way in which we relate to life is particularly important because it helps us to see future possibilities. When you are relaxed and lost in a daydream or fantasy, and you suddenly have a hunch that what you are daydreaming might come true in the future, you are using the function of *intuition*. Intuition is one of the most mysterious parts of the mind, because it allows us to understand things without having to analyse them. Very intuitive people are often very creative. A man who suddenly has the idea of setting up a business to sell a product, which he has a hunch will be important in five years' time, is using intuition.

Sometimes you may have had the experience of meeting another person and knowing a lot about him without his having told you anything. It is as though your mind registered all kinds of subtle things — the way he stands and speaks and dresses and looks at you — and unconsciously you add all these things together and suddenly know what sort of person he is. If someone asks you, you might not be able to tell how you arrived at your conclusion; it was all done in the unconscious. Intuition is also called *perception through the unconscious* because it means picking up all kinds of things and seeing instantly what they add up to and where they are going, without being aware of all the intermediate steps.

We all have sensations, thoughts, feelings and intuitions. But we are different in the way we use these parts of the mind. Some people are happier relating through their feelings, and others are happier relating through their thoughts. Introverts are happier exploring their own inside world, while extroverts are happier having lots to do in the outside world. Each person is unique, and it is important to accept yourself whatever your way is of seeing life. It is also very important to recognise that although others may be different from you, and see things differently, the world another person sees is the real one for him if he is being true to himself.

It is natural, then, that we will value most those things which relate to the part of the mind we are best able to use. We should always have the courage to seek what we value most. But we also need the tolerance to realize that not everyone shares our values. A thinking type of person may value learning and logic, while a feeling type may value his home and family more. A sensation type may value money and achievement, while an intuitive type may value his visions of the future. They are all right.

Conflict

Even inside one person, thoughts and feelings will sometimes not agree with each other, or a hunch or intuition will conflict with what our senses tell us. Every person sometimes experiences these inner conflicts. For example, you might have a teacher whom you do not like very much. But she may be a very good teacher who can really help you to learn. Your thoughts tell you to work hard at your schoolwork because it will help you to succeed later in life. But your feelings tell you that you just don't like that person and would much rather be somewhere else! Somehow you have to learn to live with both. Or you may have a hunch that you have some talent at design, and you would like to try studying it to see if you are right. But everyone in your family has always studied science and the facts of the situation tell you that you could easily get a job in the scientific field with the family's help.

Conflicts like this are a part of living. When we are young, these conflicts seem black and white. It is often just a matter of choosing the right thing to do. But as we get older, it is more important to see that both sides may be right, and it takes a lot of self-knowledge to do the thing which can blend both sides. Psychology has taught us that conflict is healthy and a natural part of life. People are never always the same. We are learning that a *crisis*, a situation that causes conflict, is often very good for the growth of the mind, because it is a wonderful opportunity to learn. We should never be afraid of conflicts. They help us to find out who we are and what we really think and feel about things.

The original conflict. Should he eat the apple, or shouldn't he?

Subpersonalities

It helps us to understand how very complicated our minds are by imagining that we have many different little people inside us, which some psychologists call *subpersonalities*. They exist underneath the behaviour we show to the outside world. Sometimes these people get along with each other, and sometimes they don't. But they are all part of each of us, and they are really all helpful and constructive even if they sometimes seem to cause conflict. The more we learn about these little people, the more we can help these different parts of ourselves to live in harmony with each other.

Try imagining some of these little people which live inside your mind. Perhaps you might find one who is a strong, courageous leader who wants to be successful in life. There might also be a shy and sensitive poet who has beautiful visions. You might also find a steady, earthy person who enjoys good food and nature and the peace of the countryside.

What imaginary people can you find inside yourself? Try taking four of them and drawing a picture of each of them. Then try thinking about whether all of them are being given a chance to be expressed in your life. If any of them are being held inside, because you are afraid someone will disapprove or dislike you, you can make yourself very unhappy. Even if some of these inside people seem bad to you, they might contain some good qualities which are really helpful.

Try to draw pictures of these little people, write stories about them, and find out what they are really like. How can the leader help the poet to be less shy? Can the earthy, practical person help the leader to be more successful in the world? This is learning to get our subpersonalities to help each other instead of fighting each other. Try writing a story about how two of your little people, who don't really get along with each other, learn to become friends.

Projection

There is another important reason why we need to get to know more about ourselves. When there is a part of us which we are not aware of, or cannot accept, it may sometimes seem to us that this part belongs to someone else. Then we react to the other person in a very emotional way, and sometimes really dislike him because of this quality which we think is his, but is really ours. This is called *projection*.

Think of what happens when you see a slide projected on to a screen. You look at the picture, which looks as though it is part of the screen. But the real source of the picture is inside the slide projector. The screen is actually blank. When we project qualities on to other people, we are not seeing them as they truly are. We are only seeing a projection of ourselves.

Think of someone for whom you really have a strong dislike. What are the things you dislike him for? Now think hard and honestly about yourself. Could some of these things secretly apply to you, a part of you that you are too embarrassed to show anyone?

Now think of someone you really admire. What fascinates you about that person? Could these things perhaps really be in you, but you didn't believe in yourself enough to recognise them?

We project both good and bad things on to others. By recognising our own projections, we see others as they really are and give them the right to be themselves around us. And we can also discover things about ourselves.

There once was a man who said, "Though
I think that I know that I know,
I wish I could see
The I that knows me
When I know that I know that I know."

Since ancient times, artists and mystics have portrayed the Self as a *Mandala*, a circular design. Mandalas of various kinds appear in the symbolism of all the world's great religions.

The Self

We have talked so far about the different ways we use the mind, and about the different people who live inside us. But we have not yet talked about the centre or core of each of us from which all these parts stem.

In some schools of psychology the real essence or core of a person is called the *Self.* This is our unique gift and our most precious possession, because it is the thing which makes us all truly different. Learning to develop this centre may even be the real purpose of life. Whatever a person does in life, his dearest treasure is his inner belief that he is worth something and that his life has purpose. No matter how much money a man has, he cannot buy this thing; no matter how talented or skilled he is, or how many friends he has, his talents and friends cannot help him to find it. In fact, no one can really tell you about the Self, because it is so deeply and specially you that no one else can really know what it feels like to be you.

We cannot explain the self scientifically. Psychologists admit that it is a mystery. Perhaps the Self is really the same thing as the soul, which in religion is the part of man that is in touch with, or is part of, God. In psychology we cannot answer questions about what the soul is. But each person's path in life seems to be organised and directed by the Self. Behind all the things which happen to us there is perhaps a hidden meaning which we can discover by ourselves if we take each experience as an opportunity to understand ourselves better. Everything that happens to us, both inside and out, seems to be part of an unfolding plan which comes from a very deep place in the centre of each person. This very deep centre may have wisdom and purpose far beyond what we realize, and recognising this can help us to live happier and more fulfilling lives.

Pathways into the mind

There are three very important ways in which we can get a glimpse of the wonderful energy working at the centre of each one of us. These pathways into the mind are also very helpful to get greater understanding about how we think and feel about things. They can also be fun.

One of these ways is through our *dreams*. Dreams are very important in the study of the mind. We know that everyone dreams each night, whether we remember our dreams or not. We also know from many scientific experiments that it is normal and healthy to dream, because people who are constantly woken up and not allowed to finish their dreaming begin to become very nervous and disturbed after a few weeks of this kind of test. So dreams are necessary to the health of the mind.

There are many opinions about what dreams really are. Some dreams are probably responses of the body to things like heat and cold and other things affecting our bodies during sleep. This causes the mind to create images. If you are very hot while you are sleeping, you might dream of sitting in front of a hot roaring fire!

Some dreams are a way of working out feelings which have not been expressed during the day. For example, if you saw something in a shop window which you really wanted, but you weren't able to buy it, your desire might be so strong that you might have a dream it is really yours.

Dreams may sometimes also be symbolic messages from the unconscious telling us things about ourselves which we have not realized.

Let us take an example of a *symbol*. A country's flag can have great emotional meaning to a person. When he sees the flag he may feel stirred, and may think of all the wonderful things he loves about his country. He could never really express in words what all these deep feelings are, but the flag expresses them much better than any attempt at words. The flag is a symbol of his country.

In the same way, all the pictures in a dream really can have symbolic meaning, and are not as silly as they seem when we wake up. The part of the mind which creates dreams does not work in the same way as our minds when we are awake. It is probable that all the different pictures in our dreams, including other people whom we dream about, are really all symbols of different parts of ourselves. In other words, each dream tells us a story about ourselves.

In ancient times, it was thought that dreams were sent by the gods to tell man how to live his life better. Perhaps this is not so far from the truth.

Another way of looking into the mind is through *fantasy*. Fantasy is often called daydreaming. We are taught that it is lazy to have daydreams. But we all do it, and many of our fantasies are important because they allow us to experience things which we cannot live out for practical reasons. Fantasies can also be very creative, and artists must picture their work in fantasy before they can sit down and paint it or write it.

Fantasies are especially important for children because they are the stuff out of which we build the personalities we will have later in life. Many children have imaginary playmates when they are young, and although a parent may say this is silly because your playmate is imaginary, he is also very real in the sense that he is expressing something for you. If you can find out what he is doing that you would really like to do yourself, then you can use this fantasy to help you know yourself better.

If we can learn to understand our fantasies, this is very helpful to the mind because, to some part of us, fantasies are real. People can become upset or depressed over a fantasy as easily as they can over an actual event. Fantasy is creative, and we should never be embarrassed or ashamed of the fact that we daydream. Sometimes the solution to a problem comes in a fantasy, after we have tried very hard to solve it in other ways. Think of a problem which you have right now, and instead of straining your mind to think of a solution, let your unconscious give you a series of pictures in fantasy which might help you to solve it.

We can also use fantasy to help us get out of moods or bad feelings. If you are in a bad mood, and you don't know why and can't stop it, try imagining what the mood might look like. Is it a frightening monster, or a nasty person? If your mood could talk to you, what would it say? Try drawing your mood, or imagining that it can tell you what it wants, so that you can understand your feelings better. Moods come from the unconscious. When you do these things, it is helpful to be able to talk to your parents about them, because fantasy is so private and subtle that it is sometimes very difficult to understand what the unconscious is really expressing.

A third and very important way of discovering the inner workings of the mind is through *creativity*. When we create something which is unique and special, we can get a glimpse of something wonderful inside us. When you paint a picture, no one else can ever create one exactly like it. It is an expression of your own self. There are many ways of being creative, but among them some of the most helpful for understanding the mind better are painting, music, dancing, and acting out stories, fairy tales, and fantasies in little plays.

An important thing which we should never forget about the mind is that it needs to play sometimes. Creativity often comes from play, and it does not matter what age a person is. The mind, along with doing all the serious jobs of keeping our bodies alive and keeping us aware of life, must also have fun, and we do this through play.

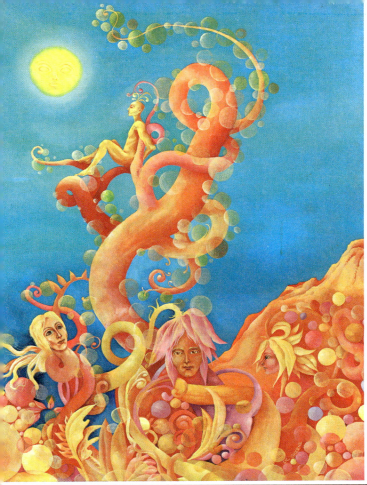

Surrealistic art, as shown in these paintings, is often painted directly from the unconscious fantasies of the artist. During the 1930's after Freud's great discoveries had shaken the scientific establishment, surrealism was especially popular. Notice the strange, eerie, magical quality in these paintings.

Conclusion

We have only touched on a few of the wonderful complex workings of the mind in this book. There are many books on psychology, and new books are being written all the time as we discover more about the human mind. There is a great deal of research and work and understanding yet to come. There seems to be no limit to outer space, and there also seems to be no limit to inner space.

You could make your own contribution to the exploration of inner space by getting together with a group of friends who are interested in self-awareness, and discuss the ideas in this book. Try comparing each others' dreams, and see if you can understand what they might mean. Or compare the little people inside you with those of your friends. Are you an extrovert or an introvert? What part of the mind do you think you relate with most strongly? And what can you learn from those who are different from you?

Many people, both ancient and modern, have believed that our purpose in life is to grow and realize ourselves. The field of study which we call psychology touches very close, in its deeper work, to our oldest and most sacred beliefs about God and about the meaning of life. Although psychology is a science and cannot really give absolute answers to these deeper questions, certainly when we study the mind we are led over and over again, like the ancient philosophers, to believe that in the mind of man there is something truly divine.

Acknowledgements

The quotation on page 21 is by Alan Watts.
For permission to use copyright illustrations the publishers wish to thank the following:
Kaspar Birkhäuser of Basel, Switzerland for the painting by Peter Birkhäuser on page 26 (bottom).
The Courtauld Institute Galleries, London, for the painting of 'Adam and Eve' by Lucas Cranach the Elder on page 17.